Meditation for Christians

Paul Connors

Book design and production by VandiDesign

Published by: VandiDesign, Meerweg 112 9752 JL Haren, The Netherlands

CONTENTS

1. Introduction

Psalms 119:15 - I will meditate in thy precepts, and have respect unto thy ways.

Many Christians believe that meditation is something they should not practice. They think it is something that comes out of other religions, like Buddhism and Hinduism and should therefore not be practiced by a good Christian.

However, many modern scientific studies have shown that a daily meditation practice can be very good for you. It improves mental and physical health and helps you to become a more calm and balanced person.

I believe that even in Christianity there used to be meditational practices. Monks used to meditate over bible passages during their eight hours of prayer (the ora et labora), and praying itself can be considered a form of meditation.

So in this book, I have taken out all references to other religions. You won't be asked to chant 'Om's' or hear things about 'chakra's. It is just a simple guidebook to start meditating and to learn to focus on the present. We will use some scripture to help us with it.

2. Sitting down

Psalms 1:2 - But his delight [is] in the law of the LORD; and in his law doth he meditate day and night.

This is a great and simple exercise to start meditating. Everything you normally do on automatic, like sitting and walking, you can use as a mindfulness exercise.

Goal:

- Getting used to taking some time to clear your head

Time:

- 7 Minutes max. I'm just trying to get you used to meditation.

Steps:

1. Find a quiet place with a comfortable chair where you

will not get disturbed. It can be at home, somewhere at work or even outside.

2. Turn off all notifications on your phone. Tell your family members or flat mates you don't want to be disturbed

3. Sit down in a comfortable position for you

4. Set a timer for 7 minutes. It is important to set this timer, so you won't be tempted to look at the clock

5. Close your eyes

6. Try to clear your mind. Focus on the feeling of sitting. Feel the chair against your body. Notice gravity pulling you down. Feel the air around you. Feel the love of the Lord inside you. Focus completely on the moment you are in.

7. You will notice it is very hard to do this. Every time, thoughts enter your brain. This is ok. Gently acknowledge these thoughts and let them pass.

8. Continue until the seven minutes are up, open your eyes and continue with your day.

3. Focus on your Breath

Psalms 19:14 - Let the words of my mouth, and the meditation of my heart, be acceptable in thy sight, O LORD, my strength, and my redeemer.

You can use breathing for an excellent mindfulness exercise. Breathing is something your body always does. By focusing on your breath, you will, with practice, be able to clear your mind.

I want to remind you that there is no perfect mindfulness exercise. Everybody is different and in this guide, I want to make you experience different ways of meditating. After, you can decide which exercise works best for you and start incorporating it in your daily meditation practice.

Goal:

- Using focus on your breath to clear your mind.

Time:

- 10 Minutes max. 20 minutes if you are more experienced.

Steps:

1. Find a quiet place. Put yourself in a position that you find comfortable. Some people like to sit upright, some people like to lie down on their back. Find out what works best for you
2. Set a timer for 10 minutes, 20 if you are more experienced.
3. Start noticing your breathing. How is it at this moment?
4. Try breathing in deep from your stomach. Relax, loosen your stomach and breath in and out slowly.
5. Put a hand on your stomach. Relax your stomach muscles so you feel it in your hand. Breath in and out slowly. Feel your hand going up and down. Focus on this breath.
6. Count your breaths until 10. When you reach 10, start over.
7. When you get distracted, or thoughts come into your brain, just let them go and go back to focusing on your breath

Don't get upset if your mind keeps wandering all the time. This is very normal. Just gently bring your focus back to your breathing and the feeling of your hand going up and down on your midriff. There is no 'winning' in meditation. Even if you only manage to empty your mind for a few moments during a session, it has been a successful session.

4. Musical Observation

Psalms 104:34 - My meditation of him shall be sweet: I will be glad in the LORD.

Some people find it easier to start meditating by listening to music. For this exercise, we will use some beautiful Gregorian chant music. This music is perfect for a Christian meditation practice.

Goal:

- Getting used to meditation with your favorite music

Time:

- 7 Minutes max. You can put one of your favorite songs on repeat.

Steps:

1. Find a quiet place with a comfortable chair where you will not get disturbed. You can also decide to lay down.
2. Stop all notifications on your devices and make sure you won't be disturbed.
3. Find some Gregorian chant music you like. You might find some on YouTube or Spotify. Put it on repeat.
4. Close your eyes and start listening. Focus only on the music. How does it sound? Listen to the long, elongated notes. Focus only on the angelic voices.
5. Every time you feel your mind wandering and thoughts appearing in your head, let them go and focus back on the music.

You can also start listening to different music. I could recommend classical music. Words tend to distract you. Look for some Chopin piano sonatas or the Goldberg variations by Bach.

5. Body scan

Proverbs 4:20-22 - My son, attend to my words; incline thine ear unto my sayings.

During the body scan exercise, you will focus your attention on every part of your body. You will start slowly at the top of your head and make your way down to your toes.

This is in no way a medical exercise. We are not trying to find pain or discomfort in your body. Just focusing on how your body feels can help to bring your attention back to the present, to this moment.

Goal:

- Slowly scanning your body with your mind and learning to focus on the present.

Time:

- 10 Minutes max. 20 if you are more experienced.

Steps:

1. Find a quiet place to lie down or sit. You can sit in the lotus position or lie down with your knees pulled up. Try to sit upright if you are sitting. Don't slouch.
2. Set a timer for 10 or 20 minutes. Turn off all notifications or mobile devices.
3. Close your eyes
4. Start scanning your body from the top. Go very slowly. Start with the top of your head. How does it feel? Do you feel any comfort or discomfort there? Do you feel the air around the top of your head?
5. Slowly move down your body, first to the middle of your head. Feel the sensation of your eyes, your ears. How does your mouth feel? Go down further to your chin, your neck all the way to your toes. Go very slowly past every body part.
6. Try to time it so you arrive at your toes at the end of your session.

This exercise might seem a bit quaky. What does feeling your mouth or your eyes mean? Remember, we are just trying to get you to focus on the present and on the moment you are in. I want you to stop thinking about the future or the past. The main goal of meditation is to get you to stop paying attention for a while to your inner dialogue. This is where the proven medical benefits of meditation come from.

6. God's Love

Psalms 119:97 - MEM. O how love I thy law! it [is] my meditation all the day.

In this exercise we are going to focus on the love of god inside you. In our daily lives, we often forget the Lord looks down on us and supports us. By focusing our attention to this love inside you, you will reap tremendous benefits. You will feel more loved and one with creation.

Goal:

- Emptying your mind by focusing on the feeling of love from God inside you.

Time:

- 10 Minutes max. 20 minutes if you are more experienced

Steps:

1. Find a quiet place without disturbance. Sit or lie down.
2. Set a timer for 10 or 20 minutes. Make sure you won't be disturbed by phone, email or chats.
3. Close your eyes.
4. Try feeling a bright, glowing spot in the center of your brain, or in the center of your chest, whatever you prefer. Focus on it.
5. Imagine this Godly love to give you energy, warmth and calmness.
6. When your mind wanders away, take note of the disturbing thought, discard it and return your focus to God's love.

7. Walking

Psalms 49:3 - My mouth shall speak of wisdom; and the meditation of my heart [shall be] of understanding.

This exercise is very different from the ones we practiced before. Once you get better at focusing your thoughts at the present moment, you might be able to start doing this while you go about your daily activities. For example, you might have to walk your dog every day, or you do the dishes every day. These daily activities can become great exercise and meditation moments.

This walking exercise will get you on your way to incorporating mindfulness in your daily life.

Goal:

- Starting to use mindfulness meditation in your daily life

Time:

- 10 minutes during a walk.

Steps:

1. Make some time for a walk outside. It is better to start this exercise by walking in a quiet, natural place, but even busy cities can work.
2. Set your timer for 10 minutes and turn of your phone notifications and sounds
3. Don't close your eyes!
4. Start focusing on the feeling of the walk. Focus on the feeling in your legs as they touch the ground. Focus on your arms, swinging gently by your side. Notice the total of sounds around you.
5. When you feel you thoughts wandering away and you are getting lost in thought, acknowledge this and return your focus to the feeling of walking. Focus on the air (if you are in nature), focus on the blend of city sounds.

This is a great exercise to start doing daily, especially if you already have to walk every day. Just set aside 10 minutes for this. What are 10 minutes on a 24h day?

8. Visualizations

Isaiah 26:3 - Thou wilt keep [him] in perfect peace, [whose] mind [is] stayed [on thee]: because he trusteth in thee.

During a visualization, you construct a space in your mind when meditating. This can be fun. I'll lead you on the way with something specific, but when you get the hang of it, you can construct your own, peaceful surroundings that work the best for you.

Visualization is a great technique to master. You might find yourself longing for your constructed space in your mind. This space can become a refuge.

Goal:

- Constructing a visual space in your mind and staying in

this space, instead of focusing on your inner dialogue.

Time:

- Between 10 and 20 minutes.

Steps:

1. Find a quiet place. Assume your favorite meditation position.
2. Turn of all phones, tablets and computers.
3. Set a timer for the amount of time you want to meditate
4. Close your eyes.
5. Start focusing on your breath for a while.
6. Now, imagine a wide open space. You see green grass and mountains in the distance. Feel the pleasant temperature on your skin. There is a little church and a big tree next to it. Imagine yourself sitting comfortably under the tree. Feel the surroundings, smell the grass, hear the birds. Feel the light of the Lord shining on your face.
7. Every time your thoughts interrupt you or you notice you have been thinking about something else, gently bring your mind back to your place under the tree.

This is just one example of a space you can construct. Try to create a space that calms you. Maybe you don't the countryside, and much rather would imagine a space high on a building, overlooking a busy city. Maybe there is a calming place from your childhood that you would like to return to.

Whatever space you construct, always try to focus on the pleasant sounds, smells and view of this place.

9. Bible Verses

Matthew 6:6 - But thou, when thou prayest, enter into thy closet, and when thou hast shut thy door, pray to thy Father which is in secret; and thy Father which seeth in secret shall reward thee openly.

Some meditation practices, like transcendental meditation, rely heavily on the use of a mantra. Instead of using a Mantra, we are going to do exactly what generations of Monks in the Middle Ages used to do. What is a mantra? It's just a phrase you repeat over and over again. Instead of using a random phrase, we are going to use a beautiful verse from scripture. You can use any phrase you pick yourself. I would recommend using a verse that you personally like a lot and which message you would like to instill in your mind.

Using a Bible verse can be highly effective. Especially men seem to have a high success rate with this.

Goal:

- Using a mantra to clear your mind and stop your inner self talk for a moment

Time:

- 10 – 20 minutes.

Steps:

1. Go to your favorite quiet place and get in position
2. Turn off your phone
3. Set a timer for the amount of time you want to meditate
4. Choose a Bible verse that you like. For example, you can use: Matthew 5:9 - Blessed [are] the peacemakers: for they shall be called the children of God. Or: Romans 12:12 - Rejoicing in hope; patient in tribulation; continuing instant in prayer. Choose anything you like.
5. Close your eyes
6. Focus on your breath for a few seconds, to calm down
7. Slowly start repeating Bible Verse in your head. Try to focus your attention only on the Verse and on nothing else. Make every repetition at least a couple of seconds.

8. Every time you lose focus, bring your mind back to the Verse.

10. Mindful Appreciation

Philippians 4:8 - Finally, brethren, whatsoever things are true, whatsoever things [are] honest, whatsoever things [are] just, whatsoever things [are] pure, whatsoever things [are] lovely, whatsoever things [are] of good report; if [there be] any virtue, and if [there be] any praise, think on these things.

The goal of this exercise is to focus your mind on the good things in your life. This might be even so small as the sunlight on your face or the fresh air against your skin, but you can also focus your thoughts on your friends or family members, or on the blessings of the Lord. This exercise can be a powerful tool in your arsenal to become happier and more appreciative of what you have.

Goal:

- Focus your thoughts in the here and now on something you can be grateful for.

Time:

- 10 – 20 minutes.

Steps:

1. Sit down or lie down. Find a quiet place where you won't be disturbed.
2. Turn of your phone, lock your door
3. Set a timer for 10 – 20 minutes
4. Close your eyes.
5. Start focusing on your breath. Slow your breath down and inhale and exhale deeply.
6. Pick one thing you want to be appreciative off. For example, pick a loved one. Focus your thought on him or her. Focus on the feeling of love or warmth you get when you think of them. Focus on this feeling only. Don't let your mind wander off to specifics, like your wife that didn't take out the trash. Focus on the feeling of love or warmth only.
7. Every time your mind wanders off, acknowledge this and return it to the positive feeling you are focused on.

You can repeat this exercise often, focusing on a different person, group of persons or thing. You don't always have to focus on the feeling of love. You could also think for example of your group of friends and focus on the feeling of fun when you are together. You could focus on something in nature, like the feeling of sunlight on your skin and how good that feels.

Of course, you can also focus on different aspects of your Faith, like the God's Love, God's Creation or God's Mercy.

If you start practicing this often, you might find that you are happier and more content with your life. Often, we forget all the small and big things that make our life worth living and focus on the problems. It is good to take some time every now and then to feel truly grateful for what you have.

11. Visiting thoughts

Psalms 1:1-6 - Blessed [is] the man that walketh not in the counsel of the ungodly, nor standeth in the way of sinners, nor sitteth in the seat of the scornful.

You might have noticed that it is very hard to empty your mind during your meditations. Every time you try to focus on the present moment, your mind seems to be assaulted by thoughts. It can be hard to let go of these thoughts and go back to your point of focus.

During this exercise, we will try to acknowledge every thought that comes to your mind and practice letting them go quietly. Becoming mindful of your constant inner dialogue can help you tremendously. Once you are aware of thoughts coming into your mind, you can just label them and letting them go.

For example, if you often get frustrated or angry and you start noticing these kinds of thoughts often entering your mind, you might just label them, like; 'this is an angry thought', 'this is frustration' and then, just quietly let go of these emotions. The goal of this exercise is to start perceiving these passing thoughts. After, it will me much easier to let them go, even when not meditating. The result? A quieter and more peaceful self.

Goal:

- Acknowledging passing thoughts and letting them go.

Time:

- 10 – 20 minutes. You can also practice this exercise in your daily life.

Steps:

1. Sit or lay down in a quiet place.
2. Make sure you won't be disturbed
3. Set a timer for 10 – 20 minutes
4. Close your eyes
5. Start with focusing on your breathing. Slow it down a bit and start breathing more deeply.
6. Start noticing the thoughts that come to your head. Give them a label, like 'worry', 'anger', 'love' or 'observation'. Once you label them, let them go and focus back on your breathing.
7. Try to keep your focus on your breath.
8. If you find yourself caught up in another thought, label it again, and let it go. Return to focus on your breathing.

You might find it useful to think of your stream of thought as an actual river stream. Once you notice that you have wandered off and are caught up in a thought, acknowledge the thought and imagine throwing it in the river, where it will disappear in the distance.

12. Mindful Observation

Psalms 119:48 - My hands also will I lift up unto thy commandments, which I have loved; and I will meditate in thy statutes.

This meditation works best if you have a nice view, preferably in nature. The idea is to observe your surroundings profoundly, without attaching any thoughts or judgement to what you see. This exercise can also train you to apply mindfulness in your daily life, outside of your meditation practice.

Goal:

- Getting used to using your mindfulness practice in daily life

Time:

- 10 – 20 minutes, depending on your progress

Steps:

1. Find a quiet place, preferably outside or inside a beautiful, quiet church. Make sure you won't be disturbed.
2. This exercise is better done sitting.
3. Set your timer for the time you want to meditate
4. Start focusing on your breathing for a few minutes.
5. Don't close your eyes. Just stare in front of you, without focusing on something particular.
6. Start noticing an object in your vicinity. Start looking at it. Look at its shape, its colors. Take everything in, without forming an opinion about it.
7. Every time you feel your mind drifting, focus back on the object. You can change the object of your focus every now and then.

13. Mindfulness in the Gym

Psalms 119:48 - My hands also will I lift up unto thy commandments, which I have loved; and I will meditate in thy statutes.

This is a great exercise for fitness lovers. After experimenting with different meditation techniques, you will now be able to take what you have learned into the real world. The gym is just one example. With everything you know about mindfulness, you will be able to apply the principles to many sports, like running, cycling and tennis. The goal is to stay in the moment. Have complete focus on the present and the movement you are performing. Let distracting thoughts about the future or past go. Who knows, you might even start improving your performance.

This exercise is written for the gym, but feel free to adapt it to a sport you like.

Goal:

- Using mindfulness to improve focus in sports

Time:

- While training

Steps:

1. This is an example for a biceps curl.
2. When you start doing you repetitions, make sure you won't be disturbed. Maybe put the music from exercise 4.
3. Now, when you start, completely focus on the muscle. Imagine your mind inside your biceps. Let no other thought enter your mind, just experience the power of your muscle.
4. If other thoughts enter your mind, let them go gently, and refocus on your biceps.

Now, you can easily apply these principles to other sports. If you are playing tennis, try to focus on the ball. Let the ball be the only point of focus. Imagine your mind being inside the ball. Let no other thought enter your mind.

If you are playing against your wife in a friendly match, make sure to tell her beforehand what you plan on doing.

14. Advanced breathing

Psalms 119:11 - Thy word have I hid in mine heart, that I might not sin against thee.

In this exercise, you will learn to breath in a breathing pattern. You might find this hard in the beginning, but it is a great way to improve your breathing and meditate at the same time. You will feel invigorated afterwards.

Goal:

- Using advanced breathing patterns in your meditation practice

Time:

- 7 minutes to begin with

Steps:

1. Go to your favorite meditation spot. Turn off all phones and electronics
2. Set a timer for 7 minutes
3. Close your eyes
4. Breath in deeply for 3 seconds, slowly breath out for 12. Count in your head. Try to really exhale all the air from your lungs.
5. Repeat until the 7 minutes are past. Keep focusing on your breathing and nothing else. If thoughts come up, just let them go.

How do you feel after this exercise? There are more patterns you can use, for example

- Breath in for 3 seconds, hold for 6 seconds and exhale for 6 seconds.
- Breath in for 3 seconds, hold for 6 seconds, breath out for 3 seconds and hold again for 6 seconds

15. Everyday Mindfulness

Psalms 63:6 - When I remember thee upon my bed, [and] meditate on thee in the [night] watches.

During this final exercise, we will start applying mindfulness to your daily activities. Now, you can do these exercises everywhere you go. A mindfulness exercise is especially good to combine with easy manual tasks, like doing the dishes, cleaning up and taking out the dog.

But you can start applying the principles even to other activities, like playing with your children. If you are with them, try to really be with them in the moment. Turn of your phone, and give them your complete attention. Stay in the moment, don't let your inner monologue take you away to another place. Focus on the here and now.

Goal:

- Getting used to mindfulness in your daily life

Time:

- Try to make a list of daily activities that you already do where you could apply some mindfulness practice.

Steps:

1. Start your activity.
2. Again, turn of phones and don't let yourself be disturbed.
3. Try focusing on the present moment. If you are with your children, focus on their game, on their being or on their appearance. Don't let any thoughts disturb you while you are with them.
4. If you are doing the dishes, try to focus on this manual activity. Focus on the feeling of the soap and the water. Focus on the sounds of the washing. If thoughts come, just acknowledge them and let them go.
5. If you are driving, focus only on the traffic and the road. Don't let thoughts distract you. Feel your surroundings and be very attentive to the movement of your car, the movement of other cars and traffic lights. If you start daydreaming, bring yourself back to the present moment.
6. When you are walking somewhere, truly focus on the feeling of the walking. Feel the ground beneath your feet, feel the sky around you. Feel the movement of your body. If you start daydreaming, let it go and return your focus on the movement of walking.

16. Resources

There are many Bible quotes about meditation. Here are just a few:

- *Joshua 1:8 - This book of the law shall not depart out of thy mouth; but thou shalt meditate therein day and night, that thou mayest observe to do according to all that is written therein: for then thou shalt make thy way prosperous, and then thou shalt have good success.*

- *Psalms 1:2 - But his delight [is] in the law of the LORD; and in his law doth he meditate day and night.*

- *Psalms 19:14 - Let the words of my mouth, and the meditation of my heart, be acceptable in thy sight, O LORD, my strength, and my redeemer.*

- *Psalms 119:15 - I will meditate in thy precepts, and have respect unto thy ways.*

- *Psalms 104:34 - My meditation of him shall be sweet: I will be glad in the LORD.*

- *Philippians 4:8 - Finally, brethren, whatsoever things are true, whatsoever things [are] honest, whatsoever things [are] just, whatsoever things [are] pure, whatsoever things [are] lovely, whatsoever things [are] of good report; if [there be] any virtue, and if [there be] any praise, think on these things.*

- *Proverbs 4:20-22 - My son, attend to my words; incline thine ear unto my sayings.*

- *Psalms 119:97 - MEM. O how love I thy law! it [is] my meditation all the day.*

- *Psalms 49:3 - My mouth shall speak of wisdom; and the meditation of my heart [shall be] of understanding.*

- *Isaiah 26:3 - Thou wilt keep [him] in perfect peace, [whose] mind [is] stayed [on thee]: because he trusteth in thee.*

- *Matthew 6:6 - But thou, when thou prayest, enter into thy closet, and when thou hast shut thy door, pray to thy Father which is in secret; and thy Father which seeth in secret shall reward thee openly.*

- *Psalms 119:127 - Therefore I love thy commandments above gold; yea, above fine gold.*

- *Psalms 1:1-6 - Blessed [is] the man that walketh not in the counsel of the ungodly, nor standeth in the way of sinners, nor sitteth in the seat of the scornful.*

- *Psalms 119:48 - My hands also will I lift up unto thy commandments, which I have loved; and I will meditate in thy statutes.*

- *Psalms 119:11 - Thy word have I hid in mine heart, that I might not sin against thee.*

- *Psalms 63:6 - When I remember thee upon my bed, [and] meditate on thee in the [night] watches.*

- *Psalms 119:1-127 - ALEPH. Blessed [are] the undefiled in the way, who walk in the law of the LORD.*

Made in the USA
Middletown, DE
11 August 2023

36542513R00024